Clothes

A very first picture book

Nicola Tuxworth

LORENZ BOOKS
LONDON • NEW YORK • SYDNEY • BATH

What am I
wearing today?

Pants and
a T-shirt...

...trousers,
socks, shoes,
and a
jumper.

Look at all my different hats!

straw hat

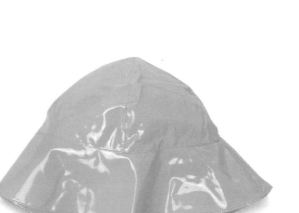

rain hat

cap

knitted
hat

checked
hat

helmet

I need to
wear my
helmet today.

I'm all
spotty…

…I'm stripey…

...and I'm covered in flowers.

He's wearing
my T-shirt.

She's wearing
my T-shirt.

I have
lost my
shoes.

Here they are.

I'll wear these today.

It's raining.

My shiny raincoat will keep me dry.

I'm a fierce
pirate...

... I'm a clever
wizard ...

... and I'm a
little rabbit.

I'm going somewhere sunny. What shall I pack?

swimming trunks

sunglasses

T-shirt

cap

shorts

beach shoes

We are in our
night clothes,
all ready
for bed.

Good night!

First published in 1997 by Lorenz Books

Lorenz Books is an imprint of
Anness Publishing Limited
Hermes House
88–89 Blackfriars Road
London SE1 8HA

Distributed in Canada by Raincoast
Books Distribution Limited

1SBN 1 85967 407 0

Publisher: Joanna Lorenz
Senior Editor, Children's Books: Sue Grabham
Photographer: Lucy Tizard
Stylist: Isolde Sommerfeldt
Assistant Stylist: Jenny Catherine Freeman
Design and Typesetting:
    Michael Leaman Design Partnership

The publishers would like to thank the
following children (and their parents) for
appearing in this book: Andrew Brown, April
Cain, Milo Clare, Tayah Ettienne, Matthew
Ferguson, Safari George, Saffron George,
Bella Haycraft Mee, Jasmine Haynes, Zamour
Johnson, Nicholas Masters, Rebekah Murrell,
Mack Nixon, James Xu.

Printed in Italy